CU01509918

A Golden Path

...Toward the Shore of Peace

ROZ WINTERS

Many of us are inner voyagers, unseen, often unnoticed in a busy world. The golden path leads us to the truth that we are all part of a vast universal movement towards the Light.
Onward...

Book 1
of the trilogy
"Portions of Infinity"

From
... A humble traveller...

Remember..

... we all have
a pre-existant
Angelic form...

Follow
The
Golden
Path...

A path opened up for me.
There were rays of golden light,
and life was woven in a fullness
beyond its clay exterior. It was
the golden light of Peace; a glimpse
of the divine Homeland.
How many have seen our true home?
I say 'our' true home because
it belongs to us/all. Our abode
of peace. And... why me? Why
was I given this glimmer of Joy?
Perhaps because of feeling homeless
all my life... always searching for
that elusive peaceful place that a
troubled childhood never gave me.
The search produced an opportunity
to enter the path of conscious awareness
The difficult childhood that once
felt like bad luck, was now a true
blessing. That was what it took to
wake me up.

Leonard Cohen sings...
"There is a crack in everything;
That is how the light gets in."

The
Lights....

It may not be obvious
at first, but for every step
you take, towards goodness
and compassion, you send
a light into the world.
The Sufi talks about Lights.
They say there are lights
which ascend and lights
which descend.
Each time a light ascends
from you, a light then
descends towards you.

Golden Light...

"My soul remains quiet"
it lives in the other world
which no-one owns.
The peach trees blossom.
The water flows."
—Li Po

... is the light of the etheric
dimension, unseen by the human
eye. Aristotle taught that this
ethereal substance penetrates all
living organisms, all plants,
animals, stone and wood.
The etheric is described as a web
because everything is connected.
Everything we do affects everything
else.
Those who possess etheric vision are
aware of the great truth that
humanity is One family.
Etheric light is golden light.
Some say that an increase in
Planetary temperature enables
invisible light to become visible.
Has climate change been set up
by higher forces?

A Revelation...

... Petals were falling from the sky. As they fell towards the ground, they floated through a shaft of golden light, and became beautiful winged beings.
When petals fall from a flower, It means the flower is dying. The golden light revealed that physical life transforms and only the body dies.
This is the truth of etheric vision. When we die, the etheric body carries us ...onward.
St. Theresa of Avila calls it...
"An infused brightness...
A light which knows
no night, but rather
it is always Light,
and nothing ever
disturbs it."

Your

beautiful

Heart...

... is connected to the heart
of the universe. The cosmos
is reflected in the pupil of
our eyes.
We are universal life
unfolding all potential
on Earth.
Like a giant jigsaw,
Each piece is a vital part
of the whole, right down
to the smallest creature.
We all play a role.

The human race is ascending.
War makes us strive for peace.
In this world of duality, this
is how we grow.
The people of the Rainbow call
the physical world's unfoldment...
"The painful impacts of a
brutal evolution of form."
Earth is where we evolve.
We are now seeing more UFO
activity as we collectively
ascend into higher dimensions,
where these beings exist.
Change is swift and darkness
is being exposed as we move
into the etheric Aquarian age...
The Age of Light

Earth

is

Ascending...

We are as a planet
raising our vibration
beyond race
colour
creed
We are all one family
We all belong.
As we awaken, we raise
the vibration of Earth
by that degree.
We cradle those still asleep,
and carry them along
Step by step.
Wars pound the Earth,
but we help to neutralise it
with our focus firmly fixed on Love

The Way...

"The great path has no gates.
Thousands of roads enter into it.
When one passes through this
gateless gate, he walks freely
between heaven and earth."
Mumon (Zen)

"Purify your thoughts.
Determine your three
worsts traits, and sacrifice
them to the burning ground."
This is the upward path.
We are here to transform
and transmute all that
is not Love.
That is why it is so busy here!
We are the universe
gathering itself
back together.

Angels

are

Everywhere...

They live on higher
Dimensions.

... you may not see them
but they are there...
a thousand wings
around each soul.
Angels can comfort us,
but cosmic law forbids
them to interfere with
Earth life.
They may wrap their
wings around us to ease us,
but cannot enter the
physical Earth plane.
Life on Earth gives us
the chance to raise our
awareness to...
higher spheres.

Suffering...

"Sometimes I go about
pitying myself, and all
the time I am being
carried on great wings
across the sky."

—Anishinaabe people

Earth life is duality,
and insight comes from the
balancing of opposing forces.
The human body is equipped
for this duality.
We have two of everything.
Our suffering can be cured.
Many teachers have lived
on Earth to help us.
They choose to return for
this purpose.
Buddha taught the
"Four Noble Truths"
Suffering exists.
Suffering has a cause.
The cause can be eliminated.
The Way to end suffering.
Become a Bodhisattva-in-training.

A Revelation...

A vast landscape before me.
Many hills in the distance
with people standing on each hill.
A powerful wind began to blow,
and many were being blown
away, disappearing...
They flew in the air this way
and that... but some did
not move.
Asking why they were still
standing, a voice said,
"because they have faith in me."
A divine Truth that our faith
in goodness/godness protects us.
The reed is flexible in the wind.
Be like the reed.
Bend with the times that you live in.

The Great
Unfolding
Cosmic
Flower ...

Unfoldment ... spirals... circles...
eternity

The One was
breathing in
silence

There was only One Power.
Then the One exhaled and a universe
was born... like glass shattering into
infinite pieces, unfolding ALL
potential.
So here we are, ancient travellers,
fulfilling our universal destiny...
bringing the pieces back together
AGAIN
The path of Return.
Then the One inhales and silence
returns.
The great turning of a universe,
Unfolding its Life.
Conscious awareness brings
the Return.

"The universe is fully automatic..."

Wisdom from a NY taxi driver! Explaining the universe in car terms.

The outer world
asks you to strive
for what you want.
The inner world
tells you that the
future will come
to you on its own.
Life follow its
own course.
How often do we
try to push the river!

Follow

Your

Heart

The voice of the heart
is a sweet refrain.
The voice of the heart
brings you peace.
The road may be dark,
the journey long...
but the voice of the heart
brings you home.
The heart only knows
Truth.
The heart only knows
Joy.

♥

Follow your heart..

Shambhala...

Olmolungring ✦ Belovodye ✦ Shangrila ✦
Hsi Tien ✦ Aryavarsha ✦
Place of Peace ✦ Dejong ✦

In 1927, Nicholas Roerich, on an Expedition in central Asia, saw a shining Round object flying overhead. Three others saw the object as it flew, then changed direction. The Lamas who travelled with him said it was a blessing from Shambhala.

Shambhala is the great powerhouse on Earth, the home of the Masters, and Very hard to find. The journey there can be arduous because it is a rite of passage, "from the profane to the sacred, from man to divinity."

Shambhala is known to be in the Gobi desert on the etheric level. It is the true centre of the Earth, and where all UFO come from. They are not from other star systems, but from our centre.

Shambhala recently increased its energy on Earth, which affects us all. This is why the system is imploding. Concsiousness!

Reincarnation...

At the centre of the universe
dwells the Great Spirit.
And the centre is everywhere,
within each of us.
Black Elk.

Imagine universal, physical
life as a large ocean; each drop
being one long stream of soul
consciousness. Within that stream,
many births/deaths have happened,
each one different.
The constant stream is the Soul,
where many lives appear and
disappear on the stream.
We are each born on a stream that
is part of a larger evolution,
the universe.
Many lives ride this stream, each
temporary, but... the Soul is Eternal
The world of appearance is an
Illusion, and as we appear and
disappear... our Soul carries
on along the stream.

A Revelation

What you seek is seeking you
Sufi

Walking quietly one early morning...
The air was warm... birds were
Chirping... a deep silence filled the Air.
The birds stopped singing...
Suddenly there was an intense light.
A feeling of euphoria fell over me,
and this small human, one of
8 billion, became part of Everything...
but there was no "part"... no "I".
The light continued to shine, and
then the words... "I just Am,"
filled the air.
The light faded and the birds began
to chirp again. It seems they too
Were affected by the light...
the dazzling light...
Spirit just Is.
Eternal undying.
Within us all, waiting
To awaken.

The sound of Krishna's flute...

"I have heard the
laughter of the
hidden host"
Fiona Macleod

Other dimensions are so close
to us. There are many ways to
touch these worlds.
Music is one way, silence
is another...
meditation...
pure silence,
walking meditation.
When you sing songs of beauty,
points of violet light may
appear.
Harmonics can invite the Christ
light.
Angel appear like white
Christmas tree lights.
Souls in this world who need
healing can also reach out
to bathe in your healing voice.

Return of of Christ...

Kindness

Compassion

Caring

Krsna

Rudra Chakrin

"In such an hour as
you think not, He will come."
Some see Christ as a quality
rather than a person; it is a
quality we can all possess.
Jesus was an initiate who
possessed these qualities
We can all be Christ if we
follow the path of Love.
A Hebridean priest in the 1800's
had a revelation of the future.
He said the Divine Spirit shall come as a Woman,
and then for the first time the world will know
Peace.
Women today are rising in
great numbers, sometimes
risking their lives by
speaking out.
Blessings to them all. ♥

*Love
is all
there is...*

"All this visible
universe comes
from my invisible
Being"

—Bhagavad Gita

If you are doing something
that does not contain Love,
you are going against the
source of life.
It is love that created the
universe
the source of power
that fuels everything,
creates Everything.
Love and hate only exist
in duality.
We are here to rise above
physical duality through
Consciousness;
To rise above the shattered glass
of physical life and understand
Oneness.
The tyrant, the sinner
are also part of the whole
When you know that physical
life is but one part of the
Divine play,
all will be bliss.

Manifesting
inner
Light...

Quietly...
study a stone or flower...
at first look at its
physical qualities.
Relax into the
Experience.
Silently, no rush,
sense its aliveness,
and connection with life.
All living things have
an etheric body, the aura
around all living things...
in the universe
This is how to manifest
Inner Light
It exists within us all
and unites us all.

Try to set aside time...
Its actually quite simple...

A Revelation...

Standing in the busy market,
a sense of expansion occurred...
indescribable really except for
an 'opening' of some kind.
The movement of the busy market
was part of it, the movement of
life on Earth in miniature.
As I stood, a voice said,
"If I die right now, I will
keep on walking."
And so it began... the journey of
discovery of the path to non-dual
awareness.
The path to the great Truth that
There is Only thing...
... and this is it being me...
... and that is it being you...

I felt my heat
beating
outside my
body...

Your pulse... blood moving
is identical to the sound
of the Earth... rotating.

... then saw
my heart
beating
outside my
body

Your heartbeat
is the same as
the beat of the Galactic
centre... 27 degrees Sagittarius

Message from the Fae...

... Our worlds is real,
more than yours.
How can yours be real
when everything dies there.
Nothing dies here
because it is real.
Look beyond your world we are not far;
Just a breath away
Look out from the corner
of your eye...
you may see us
We know Joy!
We live in Magh-mell.

This moment...
Will never come again.
This time that we live in
seems to fly faster as we age.
Spinning universes may
repeat over and over again.
Even if we return here a
hundred times more, it
will never be like this
very Moment.
Treasure your life.

At the lowest times in
our life we may receive
a blessing from Spirit.
It could be a sudden scent
from beautiful flowers
from Spirit.
(I received this when there
were no flowers nearby.)
It may be a voice that says:
"We are here,
We can see you,
We are with you."

Consciousness...

"All the centre
I met myself
waiting there
for me."

Labyrinth
Pilgrim

The greatest human leap
has been through achieving
consciousness.
All the powers that move
a universe are also moving us...
an ant... a cell... a galaxy.
Its purpose is to unfold all the
potential of the universe.
Without consciousness it
would all pass by without
us knowing.
Consciousness gives us
A window to watch it
Unfold.

Consciousness brings caring...

The

Dryad...

is the Spirit of the Tree

Dryads are often depicted
as feminine. They are friendly
beings who often come to the
aid of lost travellers. They
possess a wonderful ability
called forest walking
where they pass from tree to tree
through branches and roots
without ever being seen.
Anyone who communes with a
tree will sense the presence of
its Dryad. The ancients believed
that humans originally came
from trees.
When a tree is chopped down,
the Dryad leaves the tree.
She remains if the wood is
crafted into a harp or wand.

Brotherhood

of

Light...

It is said that there is a brotherhood
of masters living on higher dimensions.
They guide humanity from afar,
mostly through those pure souls
who can channel their messages.
These great souls are members of
humanity who have conquered
matter. We can... one day... be
what they are.
Buddha was one, and he waits
for all humanity to reach the
Light.

An

Avatar

speaks...

I asked a great Avatar
Michael Robbins, if there
was an awareness even away
from the body at death.
His reply
"Absolutely — that's where
expanded awareness really begins.
All that is seen out of the
body, on a much higher
dimension, has to be brought
into the personal brain consciousness
through continuous refinement
of the vehicles.
We know a lot more than
we know."

Heal the
sorrow
you brought
with you...

"Women will lead the
healing among the
different tribes of
the world because
inside them is the
power of Love,
strength of the moon,
and giver of life,
like grandmother
Earth."

Anishinaabe
People

You are not the doer...

"All is done
through you,
to you,
but not by you
Sri Nisargadatta Maharaj

Life is chosen. Death is chosen
But not by you...

We are all lifeforms on a
planet, and all life everywhere
follows a universal pattern
that flows a particular way...

A way that cannot be changed.
This is, for the ego, the
hardest thing to accept...

But the Soul
understands...

A Revelation...

There were many drones
in the sky...

They were following a large
sailing ship in the sky. The
Ship moved slowly as the
drones busily flew around...
and round... investigating.
Some say this is a sign of
the coming of Christ.
Many are sensing a great
occasion or impulse,
rising in the world.
The power of the ship
shook the ground.

Life on Earth
can feel heavy, as if
there is a weight (gravity)
bearing down.
As we raise our vibration
with good thoughts and
honesty, we may see the
higher world of energy all
around us.
All is Light and energy.
Could this be the true
coming of Christ
within ourselves?

All is

Light...

The illusion
of
separation

If everything is part of
the divine, then there can
be no separate parts.
All ... is the total of the
unfolding of a universe,
which evolves the way it wants...
... and this is it being you and I.
Like a great, colourful weaving
of movement, the power exhales
and a universe is born...
unfolding all potential until
all is exhausted.
Then the power inhales,
and all is stillness.
Until...
The power exhales again...

The all-seeing eye...

As soon as you ask
'Who am I?'
everything in the universe
turns in your direction.
The entire Cosmos can be
seen in the eyes of all
living creatures.

Life on Earth...
all this fuss!
The Divine power
has it all in hand.

Be grateful...

... for whoever
comes,
as each has
been sent
as a guide
from beyond."

—Rumi

A Revelation

Meeting Helena, Petrovna Blavatsky...

The door opened...
there she stood looking
very young,
and welcomed me into
her home. It was lovely,
with gold cornices on the
walls, and a chandelier.
She stood in front of me
and held out her hand,
which held a blue stone.
As she recited something
in a foreign language,
the stone began to change colour,
Then she took me to
watch a sacred play...

We are

playing...

We are playing at being the
universe, actors in her game.
She controls us so why care who
owns the Earth...
We are all actors in her life...
Her large arms bending the
strings, and if we go against
universal law, she will stop us.
What control do we have
when billions of years stand
behind us?
The universal jigsaw,
each piece vital and connecting
as we play her game.
We are in her hands
as she unfolds her amazing
potential.

You have brothers and sisters...

... Somewhere
in other
Galaxies...

... with whom you are
closely linked...

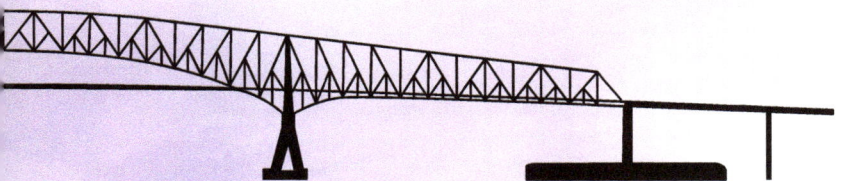

...You are never alone...

We are
the Stars...

Be humble
for you are made
of Earth.

Be noble
for you are made
of stars.

Do not feel lonely...
The entire universe
is inside you.

We Are the stars.

Buddha.

A great teacher asked
A question...

"There are billions of
bodies in the world.
We need to find out
Is there billions of "I's"
OR
Is there only one "I"
that the billions are referring to?
—Sri Ramana Maharshi

The path isn't always smooth,
but...

When the Great Love
walks with you,
it is easy to dedicate
your life to its Cause.

A Revelation...

" O light thou were my guide"
St. John of the Cross

A beautiful beacon of
Eternal Light is always there.
When asking why it did not
intervene when life was hard,
it just shone, never changing,
always there, as if waiting
for us all to rise and
BE the Light.
It wasn't just a light;
it contained All things,
All suns
All universes,
always accessible...

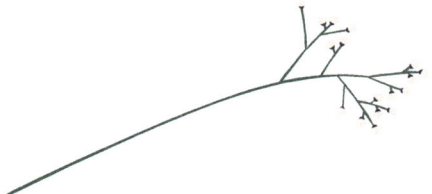

Mother...

"We are the hope of our ancestors."

Hopi

Never lose your mother...

She is your link to the
ancestral line of women
that you came from.
You follow her bloodline,
and her history will
guide you onward.
Remember the Mothers.

Eternal

feminine

spirit

carries

her own Light

within...

Keeper of the Grail...

She cares for
helpless
creatures...
... walks her
own path...

Her lamplight
shines on all...
She follows the
path of Peace...
Only she can silence
the god of war

Upward

bound...

There are 101 arteries
leading to and from
the heart.
One of the arteries leads to the crown
of the head.
Those who move upward
(ascension)
become immortal.
Those who do not,
are born again.
Transmute all that
is not Love, so you
can Ascend.

Sea and Soul...
The sea tells us about
Life on Earth,
with its neverending
movement.
The soul brings us
stillness and contentment.
Sea and Soul
the two hands of universal creation
- movement
- stillness
But ultimately
there is only One hand

Blessed

are

the

meek

Malak
means
Angel

So many displaced people
in the world. On tv, there
was a young female refugee
from Iraq. They asked her
name and she didn't know.
She was traumatized and
in shock. A beautiful child.
Her parents died in the Iraq
war. She tried to smile through
the pain. No food. She cried.
The pain of life was already
in her eyes. Her little face
still haunts me.
She did end up with her
uncle and his family.
They found out her name
Was Malak.

God bless her ♥

"The Perrenial Tradition
invariably concludes that
you initially cannot see
what you are looking for,
because what you are
looking for
is doing the looking."

Richard Rohr

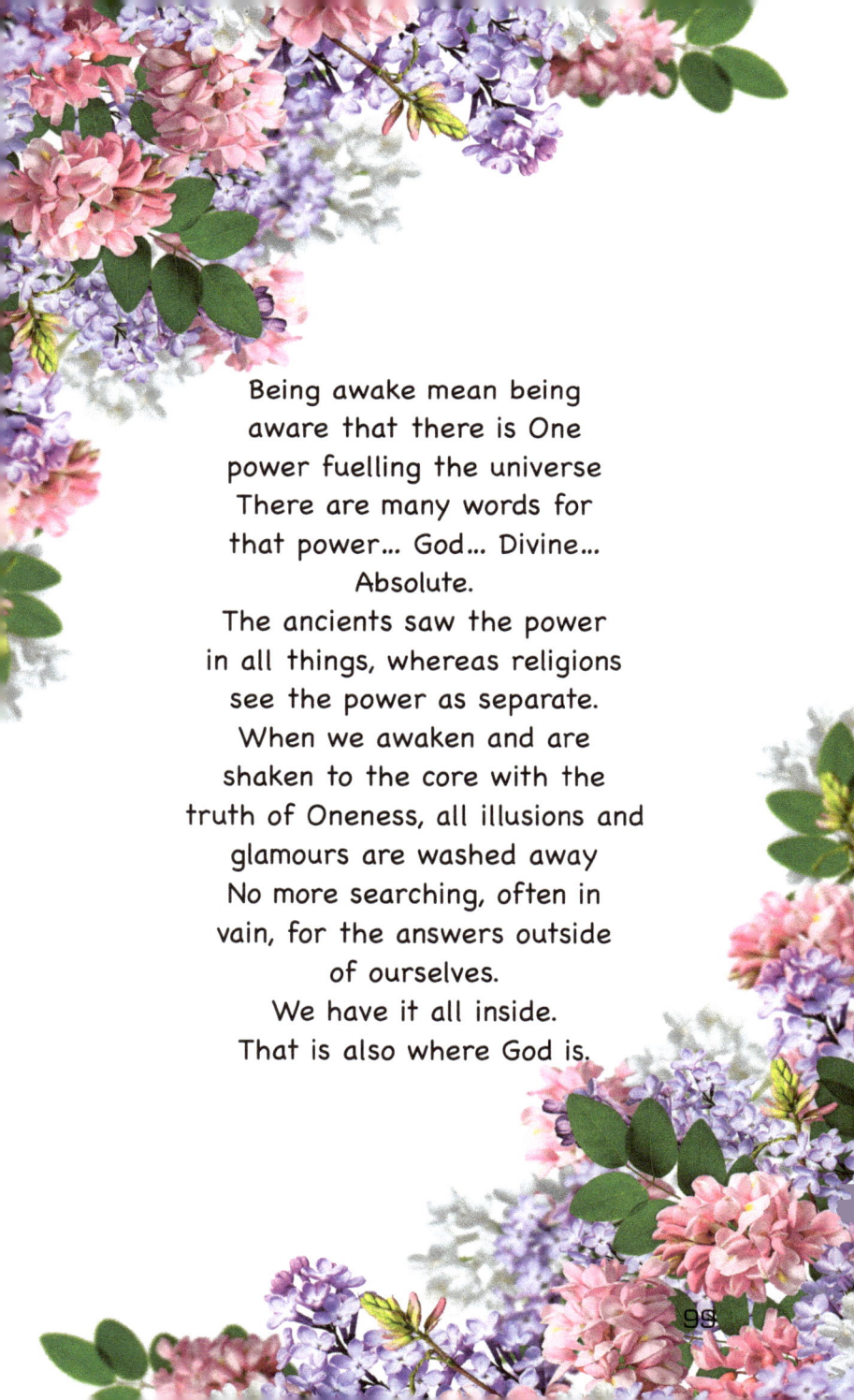

Being awake mean being
aware that there is One
power fuelling the universe
There are many words for
that power... God... Divine...
Absolute.
The ancients saw the power
in all things, whereas religions
see the power as separate.
When we awaken and are
shaken to the core with the
truth of Oneness, all illusions and
glamours are washed away
No more searching, often in
vain, for the answers outside
of ourselves.
We have it all inside.
That is also where God is.

We are like homing pigeons...

Making the arduous journey
Home...

Thirsty one keep searching,
don't give up

and one day

You will reach the spring of Peace and Love

Ascending revelation...

Letting it all go...

The past was like a dreary grey day.
A voice said, "Let it go."
"Let it all go,"
There was a stairway,
and I climbed it to visit
a friend from the past.
As I ascended, there was
on either side of the stairs,
stunningly beautiful flowers.
They were growing all the
Way up to the top floor.
The voice said again,
"Let it go. Let it all go."

Angels

are moving closer to Earth.
They hear the clamour
of war and pain.
With eyes closed in
the inner darkness
twinkling lights
were everywhere.

are near...

Streams of light and energy
are flooding the Earth
With eyes open to the outer
world, when silent and still...
you can feel the breeze
from their wings.

The perfume
of the
Temple...

When you can
smell the aroma of
incense in the air,
it means you are
protected by Shambhala
There is a sacred call
that opens the gates of
Shambhala.
Planetary alignments
show the way to a new world.
Release all that is not Love.
Then follow the Light.

Trillions

of little

Souls...

... have lived on Earth.
All fragile, all easily
wounded by life.
All looking for something
they already possess...
... already Are.
what a play!
What a stage we live on!
All playing our role
in the grand Creation.
The Creator must enjoy
Looking at the Creation
through us.
Even Hindu mystics
do not know why the
Creator made the universe
this way

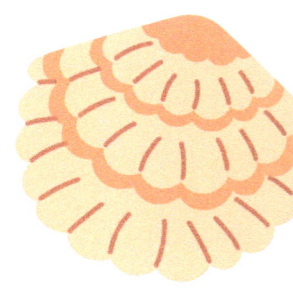

Findhorn Magic

We had spent hours at the beach
after Peter Caddy told the
community to take the afternoon
off. Findhorn beach is
covered in rocks and shells.
As we ate lunch, a stone nearby
caught my eye, so I put it in my
pocket.
The sun was warm and someone
produced a guitar and we all sang.
As we left, I threw the stone back
on the beach. Then panic!
I wanted to keep it. Where was it
among thousands of stones?
I searched and found it again!
When I awoke next morning,
with the stone in my hand, I was
being told the stone's name was
Joshua!

Findhorn certainly
was a magical place...

The plane of light

I travel to the plane
of Light, there is really
nothing else but Light.
Light moves everything.
and it is also LOVE.
We live in the duality
of day and night
the appearance and
disappearance of the Sun
on a spinning planet.
The endless night sky
contains a brilliant Light
that we cannot see.
Our eyes are filters.
Darkness is illusion.

As long are there are birds
singing in the trees,
and the long armed trees
are dancing
the world will be free.

On dark nights when we
feel afraid of war and death;
when the sound of guns
fill the world...

We can ask our God
to bring peace and caring
and pray for the world
to find PEACE.

The Ladder

It seems as I have
climbed a ladder all my
life. Each step was a major
experience of joy or challenge.
Then one day I reached the top.
It was surprising because I
could never see the top, no matter
how often I looked up.
At the top, I stepped on to a
plateau with lots of light and
a pretty landscape.
I wandered there a while.
It was beautiful with flowers
and green hills.
Then I saw another ladder!
It reached up higher
so...
I took the first step.
Deep breath... ♥

A
Shaman...

... is someone who
has succeeded
in curing himself."

Mircea Eliade

The shaman takes you on a journey
to bring back wholeness. He retrieves
the parts of you that have broken
away through trauma and pain.
The journey began at the entrance to
a cave. On stepping into the cave,
the atmosphere changed as
if in another dimension.
The cave was dark. I had a candle
and could only see a short distance
ahead. Walking on, I saw an
animal with a shiny black coat. A cat!
How sweet. Then I saw the long sleek
body and small head. A panther!
She was female. She walked ahead and
constantly looked around to see if
I was OK.
Sometimes there were moving
shadows, but they disap-
peared when they saw her.
She led me out of the cave.
She is my protector in the
dark places.

A Revelation...

The child in
the shell... 💜

While meditating at the
Findhorn community
there appeared an image
of a white shell with
the lid closed.
It began to open and
inside was a tiny baby
curled up in a ball.
This was the child I
would give birth to
3 years later.
The child appeared
days after meeting
the man I would marry.
We were in the same group
at Findhorn.

More Findhorn magic...

Love...

... has a
thousand
feathers...

Real love
　　negates the ego;
　　　　brings union with
　　　　　the Divine.

Real love
　　Releases 'me'
　　　　brings union
　　　　　　with 'we.'

Follow your heart
Everything will fall
into place.

♥

I pray...
all the lost
children will
find their mothers.
Those taken away in war...
those who ran away...
Captured like caged birds
to foreign lands,
or locked in darkness.
Please pray for them.
Rigden Jepo's helpers are here.

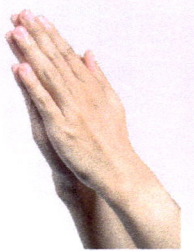

Try to remain pure
amidst
the impurities
of the world.
—Guru Nanak

A revelation...

... the song of
the universe...

Travelling through the starry night sky to a circular star system faraway.
I flew at high speed through a universe that felt cold, past planets that looked like our Earth. One in particular was bigger but just as blue, with a vivid halo surrounding it.
Our Earth has a deep resonance. but this big blue planet that resembled a choir, singing in a contralto drone as it spun.
They say space is a vacuum, but I heard sounds.
There were vortexes everywhere Onward I travelled, then...
silence.
I saw the Earth glowing
With warmth
And resonance.

The beautiful
Sufi masters...

tasawwuf

Just sit there right now
Don't do anything.
Just rest.
For your separation from God
is the hardest work
in the world.

Ayaz

Stay close to anything
that makes you glad
you are alive

Hafiz

A revelation
Of Buddha's
Light...

Visited the Buddha
exhibition with hundreds
of Buddha statues from
around the world.
The crowd moved slowly
and silently, looking at each one.
We came to a large golden
Buddha from Burma.
The line of people was long,
as we filed past one by one.
As I walked in front of him,
I felt his eyes following me!
My heart raced and my
friend Erica said...
"His eyes are following you!"
Such a beautiful piece,
a representation of a great
Avatar.

Time is an illusion...

There is no clock
in the universe
keeping time.

We follow the movement of
the sun on a sundial.
There is an experiment in physics
that proves nothing is
fixed or timed...
Physicists sent particles of light
(photons) into their apparatus.
And the experimenter decided
which way the particles went,
when it reached a fork in the
pathway. They flipped a
switch on and not only did
it change which way the
photons went, but also
changed what the photons did... in the past!
The subatomic world works
with the same laws as our world.
Time is a concept.

Sirius

A and B

It is written
that Sirius
is our Sun's star

Ancient Egyptians
knew about
Sirius
before science.
They knew its
exact position
before there were
telescopes

It could be a vortex.
Some say the
Great White Brotherhood
reside there.

Creation...

String theory suggests
there are 10 dimensions
with totally different
physics than those
in our universe.

The physical world is one of
many dimensions. It is the
only dimension made of matter.
When Creation touches the
physical universe, everything
splits apart creating...
movement.
Like shards of glass, each
piece moves away from
wholeness. This creates division
and conflict.
This may be called the
materialization of God.
The work is to bring the shards
back together again...
the true alchemical journey...

The struggle...

All through life
the struggle for me
was.. two paths
of thinking...

Does my life just
fit randomly into
the universal pattern
of evolution?
OR
Is there for each of us
an ongoing stream of
development from life
to life, within this
pattern?

Heart of
A Buddha...

In separateness
lies the world's great
suffering.

In unity
lies the world's great
strength

Buddha

When we meditate,
there is stillness.
This is our contact with
the Creator, who sits in
stillness... while the universe
endlessly moves.

The great power that
fuels EVERYTHING.
is tangible when we reach
the peaceful inner centre...
Like a swan gliding
across the lake of Being

Lots of space around
my forehead and a very
light breeze flowing through
There is a feeling of...
... vastness

... as if
the universe is in my head.
When we purify mind, body,
emotions, we can find

Infinite peace.
From the vastness of space
the body feels like
a stranger
Only Oneness Is.

I am a
stream

of consciousness within

a larger ocean...

Each of us have had many
Lives. We each have our
stream of consciousness...
the one Soul that carries us
through all lives.
Soul essence.
When the streams have unfolded
all potential within a
universe, then we will reach
the ocean
Brahma will inhale again
and all will be silent
for a time
Then...
Brahma exhales again...

That wonderful feeling
when you love everything
You can rise above
Wordly cares –

Then another dimension
appears that seems
more real...

Buddha light
is eternal light.
It knows no night
and is forever there.
It is intuition.
That small voice
that penetrates even logic.
Buddha is golden,
the etheric world
that sees all things.
Sail on..

holds the
land together

takes in
carbon dioxide

The life of Trees...

shelter

photosynthesis

releases oxygen

We are so indebted to trees,
and could not survive without
them. One mature Beach tree
produces enough oxygen for
12 people for a year.
Humans would not be here
if it wasn't for trees.
Trees remove carbon dioxide.
Countries with high populations
tend to cut down their trees for
money, so they have high
levels of smog and illness.
No trees = no oxygen
No oxygen = no life Earth
Time to hug a tree!

Searching...

for Home...

Belonging...

A little child
In a vast universe,
not knowing how she
came here...
to Earth...
Finding the way
using intuition
and warm light...

Can you feel the age
of your Soul?
Can you sense your
heart's journey?
There is a deeper life
that you are living
as the Soul is an
ancient traveller.
How many know
their Soul's story?
Walk toward Spirit
and feel the power
of the Soul in you life.

A Celtic tale
Of enlightenment...

Enlightenment is the same
in all cultures with
different stories to explain it.
Humanity is One.

Alisdair and his family lived in Galloway in Scotland. His father used to call him "the anointed man." He had a light that shone from him; a light of serene joy.

As a child, Alisdair was lying in the heather near his home, when he felt something being pressed on his eyelids. After that, he saw life very differently. Everything was radiant with lovely light. He told his family he had been touched by the Fairies with"Faery Ointment."

His father took him to town where there was squalor and slums. But Alisdair saw it only as vanishing shadows. What he saw was lovely, beautiful, with strange glory, and the faces of the people were sweet and pure and their souls were white.

"But the place is far and the hour is hidden. No man may seek that for which there can be no Quest. And there, no one alive can go... yet.

William Sharp

Angels in the Sky...

A small revelation...

Today even the clouds
are shaped like angels
and sylphs.
Wisps of clouds in
angelic forms.
Once when unwell,
sitting in the garden
resting, I felt giant
wings wrap around me.
I tilted my head to
snuggle into the
warmth of the wings.

Bondage is an illusion...

Stories from home...

Throughout my childhood there
was always a Light that
nourished me.
Grandparents were kind and gave
us shelter. My inner life
blossomed because they gave us
safety and warmth.
The golden light shone on my
Grandmother too, though her
life was hard work. She never complained.
She once said that if she came
back again, she wanted to
return as a dolphin. Free and
joyful.
I bless her each time I think
of her. I carry her DNA.
I wish I could tell her that
bondage is an illusion.
Perhaps now she knows.

The path to Peace

... is within us all.
Find your spiritual Self
and awaken the
Great Love
Love for all.
Even the antagonist;
send them love.
Now is the time.
Go Gently.

The Path of Return
within an
Eternal Universe

Joy ⟶	Source
Return to Spirit	Brahma Exhales
All worlds revealed	Universal birth
Divinity unfolding	Evolution begins
Return path	Outward journey
Brahma inhales	Unfolding potential
True Consciousness ⟵	Awakening

The Hindu cycle of time
shows the real journey of
a universe.
Brahma exhales – this is
what science calls the Big Bang
The ancient Hindu knew
this truth long ago.
But... the Big Bang theory
sees an end to the universe.
gradually expanding into cold
space and dying.
The Hindu sees the universe,
as Eternal, like the opening
and closing of a lotus flower.
Then...
Brahma inhales...

Tree magic...

Read "Man's Search
for Meaning"

Viktor Frankl

Dr Viktor Frankl was a holocaust survivor. He encountered a young woman in the camp who was dying. She was always cheerful and he asked her how she kept so happy in her situation. She told him about a small tree outside the window that she talked to. She said the tree was her friend and helped her with feelings of loneliness. He asked her if the tree ever replied to her. She said "Yes, it says...
I am here
I am life
Eternal life."

Without mud
there is
no
Lotus...

Watching war on tv.
The warmongers who try to
harness the power of the Sun.
Is this a nightmare?
Why is life on Earth a
constant struggle?
This is how the great
universal power unfolds
here in duality.
We can rise above the troubles
through understanding the
physical world and what
it is made of.
We are its unfolding
and we are striving to find
unity again
We are the universe...

Eternal

Flame

There exists in you
an eternal flame.
It doesn't need food,
sleep, or follow Time
War and pain are unknown.
It burns eternally
without dimming.
It does not age.
It has existed forever.
Being here on Earth is
your opportunity to
find that eternity.
That is the purpose
of being here.
The Creator's plan...

Then you can move on...

Revelations

...come from
dreams or
wakeful sleep.

Wakeful sleep happens as a
natural state when we can
rest the mind. It is a space
between being awake and
being asleep. When there is
silence within and without,
wakeful sleep can occur.

Shiva is the Hindu cosmic
dancer; a personification
of the creation/ destruction of
the physical universe. His dance
is the movement of maya, this
world of illusion.
His dance transforms life and
brings awakening life to
TRUTH.
When Shiva stops dancing,
the universe stops...
Pralaya.
When he begins dancing
again... Birth...
Manvantaric Dawn.

The world

is

One

Unified

**Timeless
Consciousness**

Everything...

Madam Blavatsky
describes the birth of
a universe as being
similar to a flower.
The petals open
(the Big Bang)
After all is completed,
the petals close.
This is an eternal
occurrence...
the opening and the
closing of the flower
Science is slowly
catching up to
the great
Mme B.

The great

heresy of

separateness...

Motion creates division
Without motion there is stillness
Spirit tells me...
"I just am,"
Time and space
are the Creator's
toys.

The soul is part of an
Inner Ashram.
We can visit the Ashram
in dreams and meditation,
but really... a part of our
inner being is always in
the Ashram.
Human consciousness and
outside noise are distractions
that keeps us away from
the soul life.
Using active imagination,
we can visit the soul realm.
It may be seen as a forest,
ocean, cottage. Try it and see...
the place of your Hearts
desire...
Home

boat   ocean
cottage   forest

                                  garden

What

you are...

$\rightarrow$

$\leftarrow$

What you

are not...

"Discover all that
you are not...
body
feelings
thoughts
space
this or that,
concrete
abstract.
Give up all the questions
except one...
Who Am I?"

Sri Nisargadatta

All is meant to be
I was the child
whom the teacher
thought was dumb because I
wrote backwards with my left
hand, and wrote with both
hands at the same time.
But my life improved,
making the most of my differences.
I became the kid who did
magic 'mirror writing'...
the shock and laughter when the
kids held my writing up to a
mirror and could read it!
Then I was cool!

When life hands you a lemon,
You make lemonade.

Rudolf Steiner said that
when a tiny child plays with
building blocks, and
constantly builds them up
and knocks them down,
they are copying the forces
of the universe as it creates
and destroys worlds.
The eternal jigsaw,
finding each piece to
finish the masterpiece.
Each piece vital to the
Whole.
Over and over
eternally...

I walk to the top of the
street. The choice is there,
to reach my destination
by either turning left to
wait for the bus, or turning
right to walk there
I make the choice to wait
for the bus, and turn left.
Did I really choose?
Or could it be that my mind
Tricked me into thinking
I had a choice?
Perhaps waiting for the bus
was what I had to do
all along.

"The mind is the
slayer of the real"
Bhagavad Gita

The mind is the great revealer,
but perhaps, tricks us into
thinking we are the 'doer'!
in charge of our lives.
Only the Great Creator,
is in charge...
like a cosmic jigsaw,
each piece is playing its part,
and is vital to the whole.
I can understand the world
When thinking this way.

Quote from Isa Upanishad
"Everything is perfectly
perfect in its role."

Who you are is
always whole and
perfect...
Never needing to evolve.
Nothing is separate.
Separations creates
good/evil.
Inclusion versus exclusion.
The great Creator/ God
Pervades all, and yet
Is also utter
Stillness.

Etheric vision

A revelation...
I saw Buddha
walking along
with his monks
They all carried
their bowls for alms.
Instead of asking for alms,
they held golden bowls
and handed food
to everyone
Rice, fruit, grains,
loaves, fishes.
We wait...

Tree Mothers

told me

... Keep your roots
in the Earth
for your body's sake.

Keep your branches
in the air
for your Spirit's sake.

Violet

fire...

Kundalini is real...

Woke up with lower back
pain and could hardly move.
The night before I had a
healing at a new age bookshop
I crawled out of bed, and for
5 days could not move.
My back was burning hot.
On the 5th day, I asked
Spirit about it and received
an image of a snake
belching out violet coloured fire
Revelation.. when Kundalini
is awakened, the snake asleep
at the base of the spine...
awakens.
The healing must have done this
It still affects me years later

S

Transfiguration

... a complete
change of form
or appearance
into a more
beautiful or
spiritual state...
... awaits us all...

Hearing the Great Love

Elgar – Enigma Variations
"NIMROD

Tchaikovsky – "Hymn of the Cherubin"

Ennio Morricone
"Gabriele's Oboe"

Bill Douglas
"Deep Peace"

Meeting Manjusri...

A dream...

Rising from sleep,
having had lessons
from a guru in my dream.
We were being questioned
because our teacher was
making sure we
understood
His name was Manjusri.
Someone told me today
that when you dream of
someone, it means they
want to see you

Romaju   Pinyin

              Lotus Sutra

The ancient
scriptures
say...

"the gods reside
where women
are held in
high esteem."

The face of the Goddess...

... has been
absent for
eons. Now
she returns

A new cycle is
coming, and all
tribes will once again
be run by women."
—Anishinaabe people

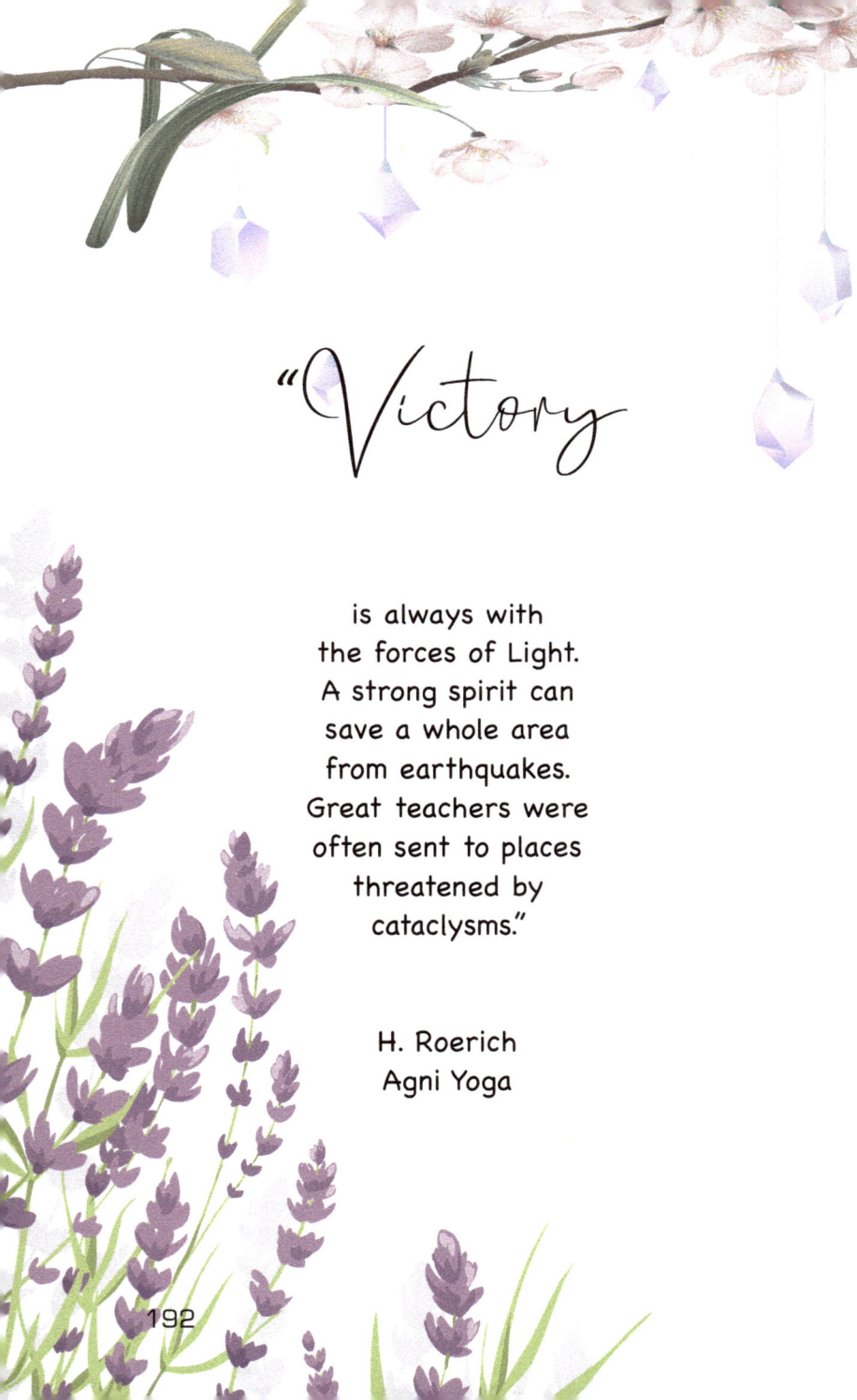

"*Victory*

is always with
the forces of Light.
A strong spirit can
save a whole area
from earthquakes.
Great teachers were
often sent to places
threatened by
cataclysms."

H. Roerich
Agni Yoga

Something
wonderful
will happen ... soon
Cosmic fire
Is touching Earth
Cleansing...
Awakening...
All will be well.

TRUTH and LOVE
always triumph

How precious...

life is on this
streaming planet
so much...
so many...
So little time to
create the masterpiece...
... and yet
ETERNITY
is
our birthright...

S

Many of us
are inner voyagers
unseen
often unnoticed
we travel
to many many
uncharted
places
What a journey it is
It is scary sometimes
But OH
the Light!

Ad asper

per ardua...

List Of Quotes

MIRCEA ELIADE – author of Shamanism

LEONARD COHEN song – Anthem.

LI PO – ancient Chinese sage, 701 AD

ST TERESA OF AVILA – 1515 AD

MUMON – Zen – 1183 AD

ANISHINAABE PEOPLE – native people of Canada. Also Ojibwe

BLACK ELK – medicine man of the Oglala Lakota people.

FIONA MACLEOD/WILLIAM SHARP – Scottish author – 1855 AD

BHAGAVAD GITA – Ancient Indian book

LABYRINTH PILGRIM – Anon.

SRI NISARGADATTA MAJARAJ – Indian guru – 1897 AD

RUMI – 1207 AD – poet – Afghanistan

BUDDHA – Indian guru – 563 BC

SRI RAMANA MAHARSHI – Indian guru – 1879 AD

HOPI – American Native Indians of Arizona.

RICHARD ROHR – American Franciscan priest

VIKTOR FRANKL – 1905 AD – American psychologist

SUFI – 2 quotes – Ayaz and Hafiz.

www.ingramcontent.com/pod-product-compliance
Ingram Content Group Australia Pty Ltd
76 Discovery Rd, Dandenong South VIC 3175, AU
AUHW011541140825
415254AU00001B/1